for Lawrence Tubb and the Wycombe Abbey Chapel Choir

When time is broke
Three Shakespeare Songs

William Shakespeare (1564–1616)

1. Give me some music

Antony and Cleopatra, Act 2, Scene 5
Much Ado About Nothing, Act 2, Scene 1

First performed on 20 March 2016 at Shakespeare's Globe, London, as part of Wycombe Abbey's 120th anniversary celebrations, by the Wycombe Abbey Chapel Choir, conductor Lawrence Tubb.

Duration: 11 mins

Printed in Great Britain

OXFORD UNIVERSITY PRESS, MUSIC DEPARTMENT, GREAT CLARENDON STREET, OXFORD OX2 6DP

4

Playful (*quasi* Scottish fiddle music) ♩. = *c.*120

*ro - yo de ro - yo de ha - ra hin - re o ro - yo

*ro - yo de ro - yo de ha - ra hin - re o ro - yo

ah

*de

*ro - yo de ro - yo de ha - ra hin - re o ro - yo de

ro - yo ha - ra o

ro - yo ha - ra o

ro - yo de ro - yo de ha - ra hin - re yo de ro - yo

ro - yo de ro - yo de ha - ra hin - re yo de ro ro - yo ha - ra o

* mouth music

NEW
HORIZONS

OXFORD

Secular
SSAA unaccompanied

— CECILIA McDOWALL —

When time is broke (SSAA)

(Three Shakespeare Songs)

Give me some music – music, moody food
Of us that trade in love. (*Antony and Cleopatra*)
The first suit is hot and hasty, like a Scotch jig, and full as fantastical; the
wedding, mannerly modest, as a measure, full of state and ancientry; and
then comes repentance, and with his bad legs, falls into the cinque pace faster
and faster, till he sink into his grave. (*Much Ado About Nothing*)

Mark how one string, sweet husband to another,
Strikes each in each by mutual ordering;
Resembling sire and child and happy mother,
Who, all in one, one pleasing note do sing. (Sonnet VIII)

Ha, ha! keep time: how sour sweet music is,
When time is broke and no proportion kept! (*Richard II*)
It is the lark that sings so out of tune,
Straining harsh discords and unpleasing sharps. (*Romeo and Juliet*)
You would sound me from my lowest note to the top of my compass… The
rest is silence. (*Hamlet*)

William Shakespeare (1564–1616)

When time is broke is also available in a version for SSATB voices
(ISBN 978-0-19-340824-1).

*if the singers lack music stands and are therefore unable to clap, they could stamp their feet, or the conductor could clap

8

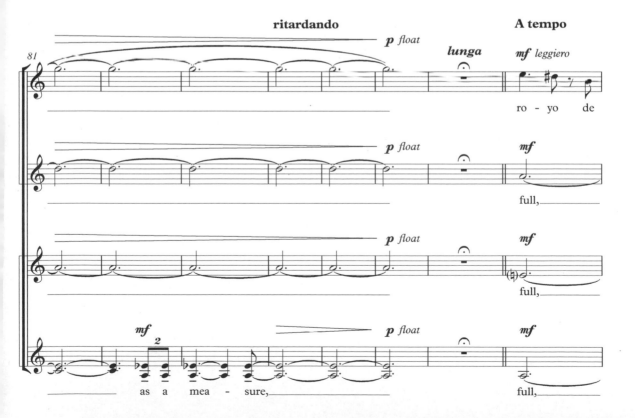

Sempre l'istesso tempo (but expressive)

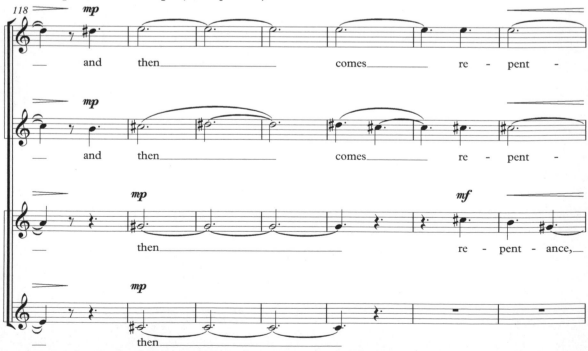

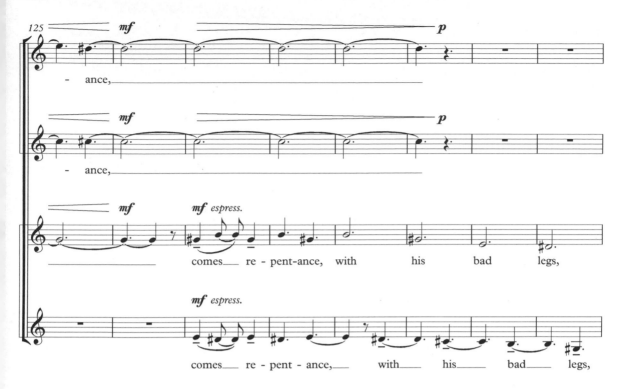

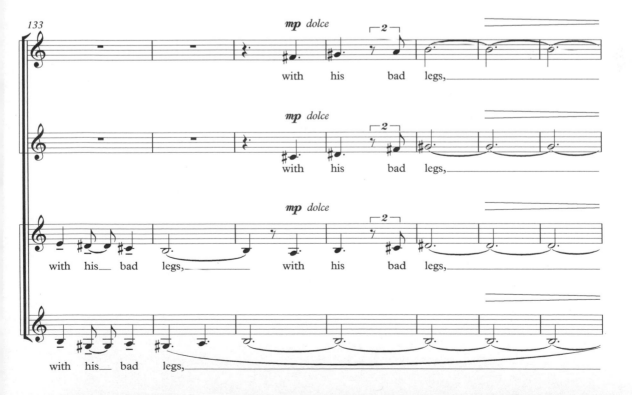

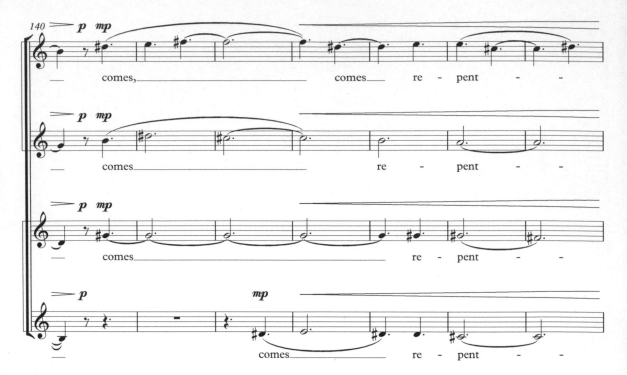

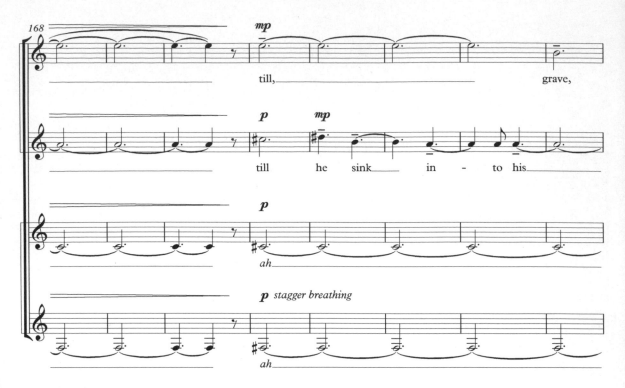

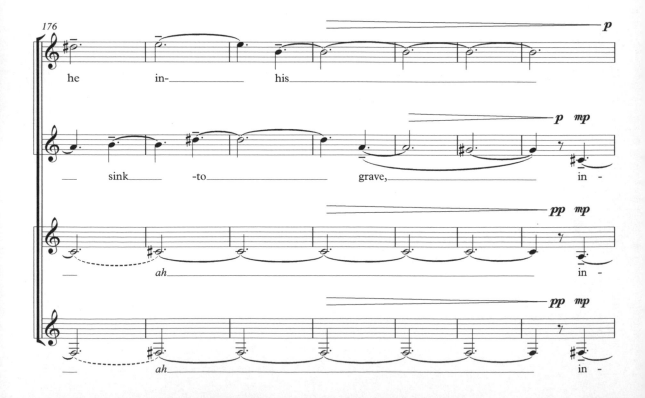

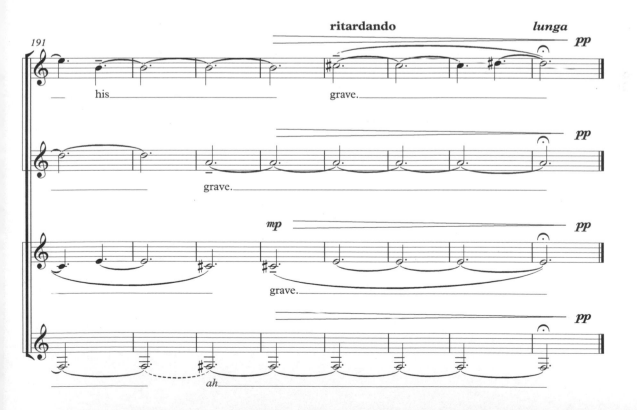

2. Mark how one string

Extract from Sonnet VIII

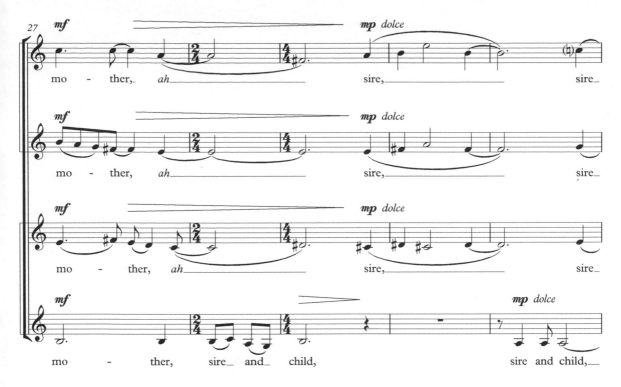

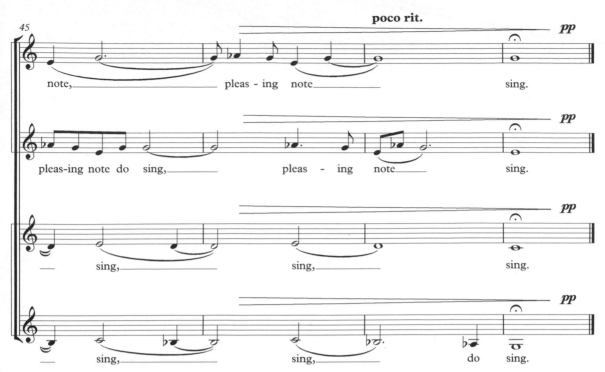

3. How sour sweet music is

Richard II, Act 5, Scene 5
Romeo and Juliet, Act 3, Scene 5
Hamlet, Act 3, Scene 2, & Act 5, Scene 2

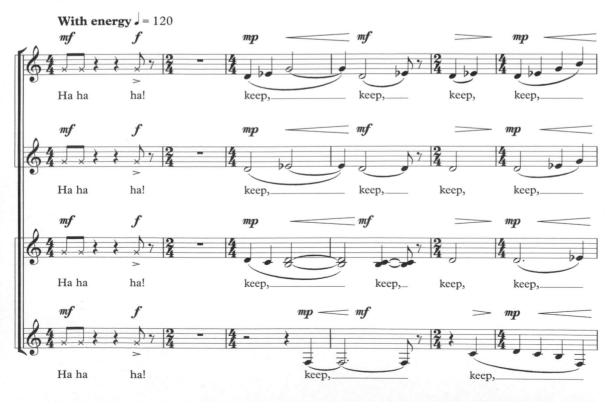

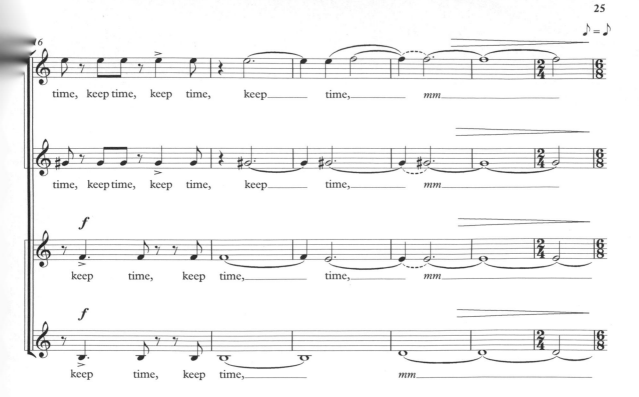

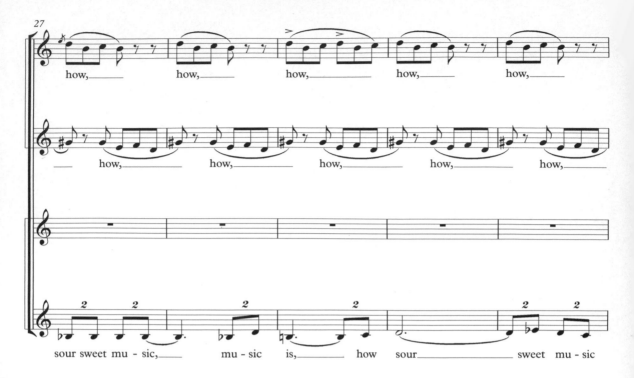

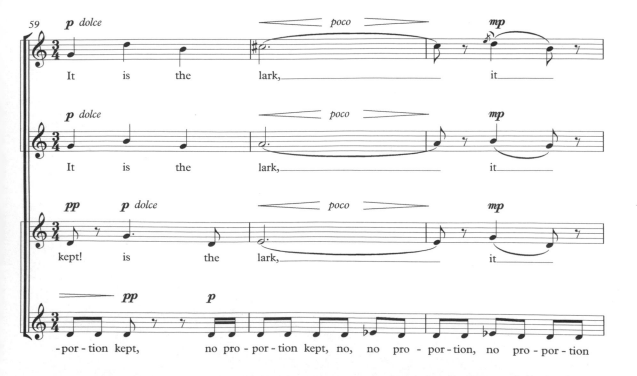

30

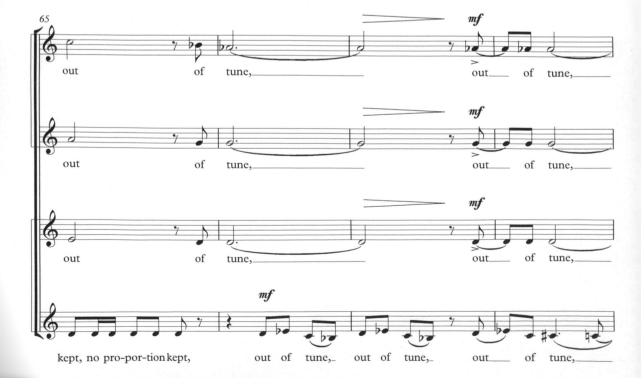

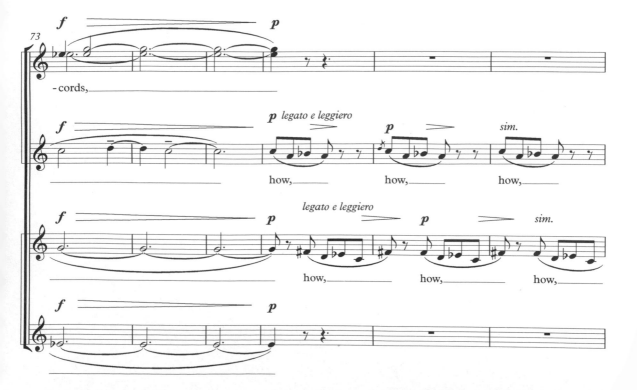

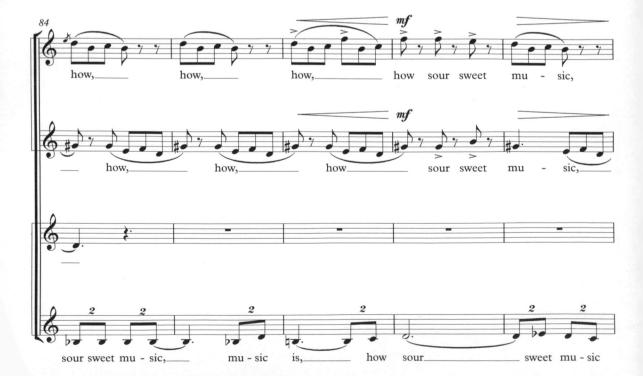

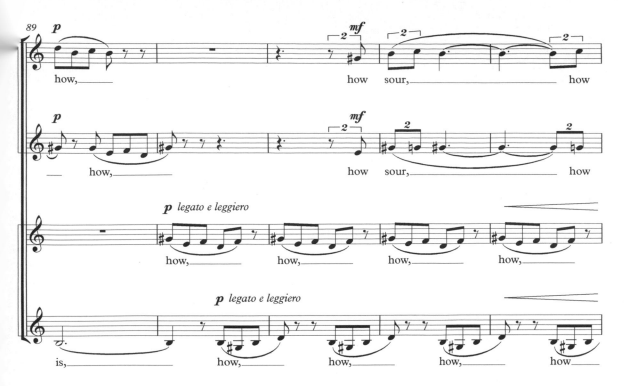

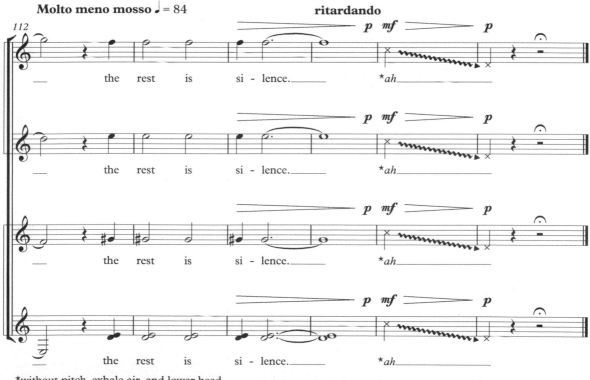

*without pitch, exhale air, and lower head

NEW HORIZONS showcases the wealth of exciting, innovative, and occasionally challenging choral music being written today. It encompasses the whole gamut of small-scale choral genres, both secular and sacred, and includes pieces for upper-voice and mixed choirs. With titles by some of the most accomplished choral composers active in Great Britain and abroad, the series introduces new repertoire and fresh talent to a broad spectrum of choirs.

Cecilia McDowall

Born in 1951 and educated at Edinburgh and London Universities, Cecilia McDowall has been described by the *International Record Review* as having a 'communicative gift that is very rare in modern music'. An award-winning composer, McDowall is often inspired by extra-musical influences, and her choral writing combines rhythmic vitality with expressive lyricism. Her music has been commissioned, performed, and recorded by leading choirs, among them Phoenix Chorale and the Choir of New College, Oxford, and is regularly programmed at prestigious festivals in Britain and abroad.

OXFORD
UNIVERSITY PRESS

www.oup.com

ISBN 978-0-19-341374-0

9 780193 413740